차 근 차 근

초등영어
교과서
미리쓰기

4학년

사람in
saram
in.com

차근차근 초등영어 교과서 미리 쓰기 4학년

저자 | AST Jr. English Lab
초판 1쇄 발행 | 2016년 6월 30일
초판 2쇄 발행 | 2019년 8월 14일

발행인 | 박효상
총괄이사 | 이종선
편집장 | 김현
편집 | 신은실, 김설아
디자인 | 이연진
마케팅 | 이태호, 이전희
관리 | 김태옥

종이 | 월드페이퍼
인쇄 · 제본 | 현문자현

출판등록 | 제10-1835호
발행처 | 사람in
주소 | 04034 서울시 마포구 양화로11길 14-10(서교동) 3F
전화 | 02) 338-3555(代)   팩스 | 02) 338-3545
E-mail | saramin@netsgo.com
Homepage | www.saramin.com

우아한 지적만보 기민한 실사구시 **사람in**

Q&A

엄마들이 꼭 알아야 할 초등영어 학습 비법

Q: 왜 쓰면서 영어를 공부해야 할까요?

A: 글씨를 쓸 때는 운동 능력과 인지 능력이 함께 사용됩니다. 스스로 몸을 움직여 글씨를 쓴다(운동 능력)는 것은 글자를 깨우쳤다(인지 능력)는 것을 의미합니다. 그 글자를 통해 자신의 생각과 느낌을 다른 사람과 나눌 수 있게 되므로 우리는 '쓰기'라는 행위에 주목해야 합니다. 영어 문장 따라 쓰기는 단순한 글씨 베끼기가 아니라 글자를 단어로 만들고, 단어를 문장으로 만드는 과정이며, 이를 통해 영어 구사력을 키울 수 있는 가장 좋은 학습 장치입니다.

Q: 쓰기 연습은 나중에 시켜도 되지 않을까요?

A: 초등학교 생활에서 글씨 쓰기는 생각보다 많은 부분을 차지합니다. 수업시간에 여러 가지 활동을 하면서 글을 쓰고, 집에서 숙제를 하면서 글을 쓰고, 얼마나 잘 배웠는지 시험을 볼 때도 글을 씁니다. 그렇기 때문에 쓰기 능력이 떨어지는 아이는 학교 수업 수행 능력에 중대한 영향을 받게 되고 자신감을 잃기 쉽습니다. 학교는 아이들이 무엇을 얼마나 잘 배웠는지 쓰기로 판단합니다.

Q: 원어민 선생님이 필요하지 않을까요?

A: 아무리 훌륭한 식사라도 스스로 씹지 않으면 소화가 되지 않습니다. 중요한 것은 공부를 많이 하는 것이 아니라 스스로 하는 것입니다. 쓰기는 억지로 시킬 수 없습니다. 몸을 통째로 – 눈, 팔, 손 – 움직여야 제대로 쓸 수 있습니다. 스스로 해야만 완성할 수 있기 때문에 쓰기는 자신의 힘으로 문제를 해결하는 법을 터득하는 자기주도 학습의 시작점입니다.

Q: 어떻게 빨리 늘까요?

A: 진정한 실력은 한 가지를 알아도 제대로 아는 것입니다. 학습을 차근차근 다지는 일에 힘을 쏟은 학생은 학년이 올라갈수록 두각을 나타내게 됩니다. 스스로 의지를 갖고 노력하다 보면 차츰 높은 수준의 사고력을 발휘하게 되고, 자연히 창의적으로 문제를 해결하는 능력도 익히게 되는 것입니다.

초등학교 시절부터 스스로 학습하는 태도를 익히는 것이야 말로 우리 아이의 학습력을 꾸준히 상승시킬 수 있는 가장 쉬운 방법입니다!

이 책으로 초등영어 교과서 문장 미리 배우기!

QR코드로 원어민 선생님의 발음을 듣고 따라 말하세요.
MP3 파일은 www.saramin.com 자료실에서 다운로드 받을 수도 있어요.

초등영어 교과서에 수록된 의사소통 문장들이에요.

차근차근 단어를 듣고 따라 읽으며 써 보세요. 또박또박 쓰다 보면 저절로 머리에 새겨져요.

차근차근 문장을 듣고 따라 읽으며 써 보세요. 단어를 먼저 알고 문장을 읽으니 뜻이 더욱 잘 이해 돼요.

쉽고 재미있게 언어형식을 배워요.

원리를 알아야 문장을 응용할 수 있어요.

쉬운 예문과 간단한 설명으로 영어 문장의 원리를 스스로 깨우쳐요.

스스로 생각하며 학습을 마무리해 보세요.

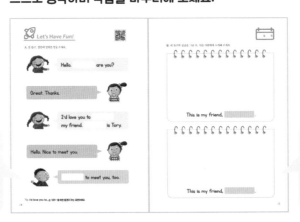

대화를 두 번 들려줍니다. 잘 듣고, 빈칸에 알맞은 말을 넣어 대화를 완성해 보세요.

그림 그리기, 낱말 퍼즐, 빙고 등 다양한 활동으로 재미있게 공부해 보세요.

이 책으로 스스로 공부하는 습관 기르기!

▶ **나에게 알맞은 학습량을 스스로 정해 보세요.**

☐ 2주 완성: 1일 4장씩

☐ 4주 완성: 1일 2장씩

☐ 8주 완성: 1일 1장씩

▶ **진도표에 나만의 학습 계획을 세우세요. 계획을 지키면 영어실력도 함께 지킬 수 있어요!**

Unit 01	Unit 02	Rule 01	Let's Have *Fun!*	Unit 03	Unit 04	Rule 02
월 일	월 일	월 일	월 일	월 일	월 일	월 일
Let's Have *Fun!*	Unit 05	Unit 06	Rule 03	Let's Have *Fun!*	Unit 07	Unit 08
월 일	월 일	월 일	월 일	월 일	월 일	월 일
Rule 04	Let's Have *Fun!*	Unit 09	Unit 10	Rule 05	Let's Have *Fun!*	Unit 11
월 일	월 일	월 일	월 일	월 일	월 일	월 일
Unit 12	Rule 06	Let's Have *Fun!*	Unit 13	Unit 14	Rule 07	Let's Have *Fun!*
월 일	월 일	월 일	월 일	월 일	월 일	월 일
Unit 15	Unit 16	Rule 08	Let's Have *Fun!*	Unit 17	Unit 18	Rule 09
월 일	월 일	월 일	월 일	월 일	월 일	월 일
Let's Have *Fun!*	Unit 19	Unit 20	Rule 10	Let's Have *Fun!*	Unit 21	Unit 22
월 일	월 일	월 일	월 일	월 일	월 일	월 일
Rule 11	Let's Have *Fun!*	Unit 23	Unit 24	Rule 12	Let's Have *Fun!*	Unit 25
월 일	월 일	월 일	월 일	월 일	월 일	월 일
Unit 26	Rule 13	Let's Have *Fun!*	Unit 27	Unit 28	Rule 14	Let's Have *Fun!*
월 일	월 일	월 일	월 일	월 일	월 일	월 일

목차

Unit 01	**How are you?** 잘 지내?	p.8
Unit 02	**This is Lucy.** 이얘는 루시야.	p.10
	Rule 01 How 의문문	p.12
	Let's Have Fun!	p.14
Unit 03	**Let's go to school.** 학교에 가자.	p.16
Unit 04	**Sounds good.** 좋은 생각이야.	p.18
	Rule 02 Action Verbs 동작 동사	p.20
	Let's Have Fun!	p.22
Unit 05	**Put the paper here.** 종이는 여기에 둬.	p.24
Unit 06	**Don't eat here.** 여기서 먹지 마.	p.26
	Rule 03 Imperative Sentence 명령문	p.28
	Let's Have Fun!	p.30
Unit 07	**Who is he?** 그는 누구니?	p.32
Unit 08	**What do you do?** 무슨 일을 하세요?	p.34
	Rule 04 Jobs 직업	p.36
	Let's Have Fun!	p.38
Unit 09	**Where is my watch?** 내 시계 어디 있지?	p.40
Unit 10	**Where are you?** 너 어디 있니?	p.42
	Rule 05 Preposition 전치사	p.44
	Let's Have Fun!	p.46
Unit 11	**What are you doing?** 너 뭐하고 있니?	p.48
Unit 12	**What's he doing?** 그는 뭐하고 있니?	p.50
	Rule 06 Present Continuous 현재진행	p.52
	Let's Have Fun!	p.54
Unit 13	**What time is it?** 몇 시니?	p.56
Unit 14	**It's time for lunch.** 점심 먹을 시간이야.	p.58
	Rule 07 Telling Time 시간 말하기	p.60
	Let's Have Fun!	p.62

Unit 15	**Do you want some pizza?** 피자 좀 먹을래?	p.64
Unit 16	**What do you want?** 무엇을 원하니?	p.66
	Rule 08 Conjunction 접속사	p.68
	Let's Have *Fun!*	p.70
Unit 17	**Is this your cup?** 이거 네 컵이니?	p.72
Unit 18	**What's this?** 이것은 무엇이니?	p.74
	Rule 09 Possessive 소유격	p.76
	Let's Have *Fun!*	p.78
Unit 19	**What day is it today?** 오늘은 무슨 요일이니?	p.80
Unit 20	**We have math class today.** 우리 오늘 수학 수업 있어.	p.82
	Rule 10 Months 달	p.84
	Let's Have *Fun!*	p.86
Unit 21	**How much is it?** 이거 얼마예요?	p.88
Unit 22	**Can I help you?** 도와줄까요?	p.90
	Rule 11 Money 돈	p.92
	Let's Have *Fun!*	p.94
Unit 23	**How's the wether today?** 오늘 날씨는 어때?	p.96
Unit 24	**What's the weather like in New York?** 뉴욕 날씨는 어때?	p.98
	Rule 12 Weather 날씨	p.100
	Let's Have *Fun!*	p.102
Unit 25	**Did you have a good weekend?** 지난 주말 잘 보냈니?	p.104
Unit 26	**What did you do yesterday?** 너 어제 뭐 했니?	p.106
	Rule 13 Past 1 과거 (규칙형)	p.108
	Let's Have *Fun!*	p.110
Unit 27	**How was your vacation?** 방학 어땠어?	p.112
Unit 28	**I had a great time!** 좋은 시간을 보냈어.	p.114
	Rule 14 Past 2 과거 (불규칙형)	p.116
	Let's Have *Fun!*	p.118
	정답 및 대본	p.120

How are you?
잘 지내?

How are you?

Fine. Thanks.

Fine. Thanks.
좋아. 고마워.

How are you?
잘 지내?

How are you?

I'm doing well.

I'm doing well.
잘 지내.

How are you?
잘 지내?

How are you?

Not so good.

Not so good.
별로야.

How are you?
잘 지내?

How are you?

Not bad.

Not bad.
그냥 그래.

Tip. **How are you?**는 **How's it going?** 또는 **How are you doing?**으로 물을 수도 있어요.

This is Lucy.
얘는 루시야.

Jiho, this is Lucy.
지호, 얘는 루시야.

Jiho, this is Lucy.

Nice to meet you.
만나서 반가워.

Nice to meet you.

Nice to meet you, too.
나도 만나서 반가워.

Nice to meet you, too.

Hi, let me introduce my friend.

안녕. 내 친구를 소개해 줄게.

Hi, let me introduce my

friend.

Hi, my name is Bora.

안녕. 내 이름은 보라야.

Hi, my name is Bora.

Hi, I'm Tori. Happy to meet you.

안녕, 나는 토리야. 만나서 기뻐.

Hi, I'm Tori. Happy to meet

you.

Tip. this는 물건을 가리킬 때 는 '이것', 사람을 가리킬 때는 '이 사람, 이애'라는 뜻이 된답니다.

 **Rule 01.** How

How are you? (너) 잘 지내니?

▶ How는 '어떻게'라는 뜻으로 다른 사람의 상태를 물을 때 써요.

A. 다른 사람의 상태를 물어보는 문장을 만드세요.

How	is / are	주어	?

1. you

How	are	you	?

2. he

3. they

4. she

Tip. 주어에 따라 is 또는 are를 써요. she – is / he – is / you – are / they – are

How do you ski? 너는 어떻게 스키 타니?

▶ How는 '어떻게'라는 뜻으로 어떤 것을 하는 방법을 물을 때도 써요.

B. 다음을 참고하여 어떤 것을 하는 방법을 물어보세요.

How do / does 주어 동사 ?

1. you / sing

How do you sing ?

2. he / run

3. he / study

4. they / walk

Tip. 주어에 따라 do 또는 does를 써요. you – do / they – do / she – does / he – does

13

 **Let's Have *Fun!***

A. 잘 듣고, 빈칸에 알맞은 말을 쓰세요.

Hello. [_____] are you?

Great. Thanks.

I'd love you to [_____] my friend. [_____] is Tory.

Hello. Nice to meet you.

[_____] to meet you, too.

Tip. I'd love you to...는 '네가 ~을 하면 좋겠다'라는 표현이에요.

14

B. 내 친구의 얼굴을 그린 후, 다른 사람에게 소개해 보세요.

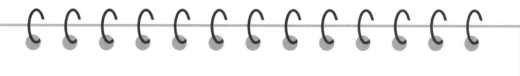

This is my friend,   .

This is my friend,   .

Let's go to school.
학교에 가자.

let's

~하자

go

가다

home

집에[으로], 집

school

학교

to school

학교에

play

(운동 · 경기 등을) 하다

soccer

축구

baseball

야구

무엇을 하자고 제안할 수 있어요.

Let's go home.

집에 가자.

Let's go home.

Let's go to school.

학교에 가자.

Let's go to school.

Let's play soccer after school.

방과 후에 축구를 하자.

Let's play soccer after

school.

Let's play baseball next weekend.

다음 주말에 야구를 하자.

Let's play baseball next

weekend.

Sounds good.
좋은 생각이야.

제안에 답할 수 있어요.

Let's go hiking.
하이킹 가자.

Let's go hiking

Sounds good.

Sounds good.
좋아. 고마워.

Let's play soccer.
축구하자.

Let's play soccer.

Sorry, I'm tired.
미안하지만, 나 피곤해.

Sorry, I'm tired.

How about baseball?

야구 어때?

How about baseball?

Okay.

Okay.

좋아.

Let's go shopping.

쇼핑하러 가자.

Let's go shopping.

Great.

Great.

좋아.

Tip. **Sounds good.** 에서는 앞에 **It**이 생략됐어요. 회화에서는 이렇게 **It**을 빼고 얘기하기도 해요.

Rule 02. Action Verbs

go   play   eat   sing   laugh

가다   (악기를) 연주하다   먹다   노래하다   웃다

▶ 동사는 누군가 또는 무언가의 움직임을 나타내요.

※ 動 움직일 동, 詞 말씀 사

A. 다음 문장에서 동사를 찾아 쓰세요.

1. James eats a pizza.

➡

2. Hans laughs loudly.

➡

3. My family goes to church.

➡

4. Suho plays the violin.

➡

5. Jina sings a song every day.

➡

B. 다음 장소에서 여러분이 하는 동작들을 아래 상자에서 찾아 써 보세요.

at school

at home

at a park

at a restaurant

run	order	eat	wait	talk
sleep	sing	dance	cook	pay
wash	listen	read	play	study
sit	stand	watch	meet	ride

Tip. 영어사전에서 단어의 뜻을 찾아보세요.

Let's Have *Fun!*

A. 잘 듣고, 빈칸에 알맞은 말을 쓰세요.

Let's [ ] soccer.

[ ] good.

[ ], I can't.
I have a cold.

That's too [ ].

I hope you get well soon.

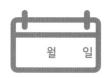

B. 그림에 알맞은 스포츠를 써 넣어 낱말 퍼즐을 완성하세요.

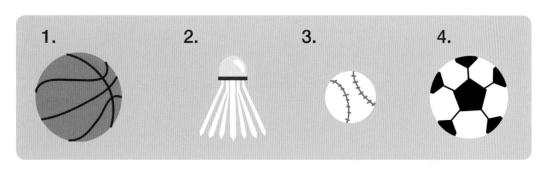

Put the paper here.
종이는 여기에 둬.

put

(특정한 장소 · 위치에) 놓다[두다/넣다/얹다]

paper

종이

bottle

병

wash

씻다

a hand

손

hands

손들

a foot

발

feet

발들

지시할 수 있어요.

Put the paper here.

종이는 여기에 둬.

Put the paper here.

Put the bottle here.

병은 여기에 둬.

Put the bottle here.

Wash your hands.

손을 씻어라.

Wash your hands.

Wash your feet.

발을 씻어라.

Wash your feet.

Tip. 손발을 씻을 때는 양손, 양발을 씻는 거라서 hands(손들), feet(발들)이라고 씁니다.

Don't eat here.
여기서 먹지 마.

Don't ~

~하지 마

eat

먹다

run

뛰다

talk

이야기하다

laugh

웃다

하지 마라고 할 수 있어요.

Don't eat here.

여기서 먹지 마.

Don't eat here.

Don't run here.

여기서 뛰지 마.

Don't run here.

Don't talk.

말하지 마.

Don't talk.

Don't laugh.

웃지 마.

Don't laugh.

> # Wash your hands. 손을 닦아.
> # Please wash your hands. 손을 닦으세요.
>
> ▶ 동사를 문장 맨 앞에 쓰면 다른 사람에게 무엇을 하라고 지시하는 **명령문**이 돼요.
> 문장의 앞이나 뒤에 **please**를 붙이면 좀 더 공손한 느낌이 들어요.

A. 동사와 알맞은 단어들을 연결하여 명령문을 만들어 보세요.

1. **Wash** ●   ● **the book.**
   얼굴을 씻어.

2. **Study** ●   ● **your face.**
   매일 영어 공부해.

3. **Read** ●   ● **English every day.**
   그 책을 읽어.

4. **Clean up** ●   ● **to school.**
   식탁을 치워.

5. **Go** ●   ● **the table.**
   학교에 가.

28

Don't eat here. 여기서 먹지 마.

Please don't eat here. 여기서 먹지 마세요.

▶ 「Don't +동사」를 문장 맨 앞에 쓰면 다른 사람에게 무엇을 하지 말라고 금지하는 **명령문**이 돼요.
문장의 앞이나 뒤에 please를 붙이면 좀 더 공손한 느낌이 들어요.

B. 다음을 금지하는 말로 바꾸세요.

1. Wash your face.

➡ _____

2. Study English every day.

➡ _____

3. Read the book.

➡ _____

4. Clean up the table.

➡ _____

5. Go to school.

➡ _____

Let's Have *Fun!*

A. 다음을 듣고 빈칸에 알맞은 말을 쓰세요.

People make this park dirty.

Let's [   ] up.
Help me, please.

Okay. I'll [   ].

Thanks. [   ] the paper
cups here.

Don't touch these bottles.
They're broken.

I can handle it.

[   ] do that. We need
gloves.

30

B. 그림을 보고 선생님이 할 명령문으로 알맞은 것을 찾아 기호를 쓰세요.

ⓐ Be quiet!

ⓑ Keep your mobile phone in your schoolbag!

ⓒ Go to the board!

ⓓ Sit down!

ⓔ Open your notebook!

ⓕ Raise your hand!

1.

2.

3.

4.

5.

6.

Who is he?

그는 누구니?

a teacher

선생님

a doctor

의사

a pilot

조종사

Who is ~?

~는 누구니?

누구인지 묻고 답할 수 있어요.

Who is he?
그는 누구니?

Who is he?

He's a teacher

He's a teacher.
그는 선생님이야.

He is a doctor

He is a doctor.
그는 의사야.

Who is she?
그녀는 누구니?

Who is she?

She's a pilot

She's a pilot.
그녀는 조종사야.

33

What do you do?

무슨 일을 하세요?

what

무엇

do

~을 하다

a cook

요리사

a firefighter

소방관

직업을 묻고 답할 수 있어요.

What do you do?

무슨 일을 하세요?

What do you do?

I'm a cook.

I'm a cook.

나는 요리사야.

What does she do?

그녀는 무슨 일을 하나요?

What does she do?

She's a firefighter.

그녀는 소방관이야.

She's a firefighter.

Tip. **What do you do?에서 첫 번째 do는 의문문을 만드는 데 쓰였을 뿐 특별한 뜻이 없어요.
이것은 뒤에 오는 주어에 따라 do 또는 does가 돼요.**

Rule 04. Jobs

A. 다양한 직업을 알아보아요.

a teacher

a vet

a scientist

a pilot

a police officer

an athlete

a musician

a firefighter

a doctor

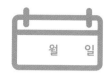

B. 장소와 그곳에서 일하는 사람을 바르게 연결하세요.

1. an airport ●   ●

2. a school ●   ●

3. a police station ●   ●

4. a fire station ●   ●

5. an animal hospital ●   ●

Let's Have *Fun!*

A. 잘 듣고, 빈칸에 알맞은 말을 쓰세요.

[_____]! I can't believe he is here.

Who? Do you mean the guy surrounded by the girls?

[_____]. He's looking at me.

Well, I don't thinks so.
[_____] is he?

Don't you know Tom?
He's a famous [_____].

B. 나는 누구인지 맞추고, 그림으로 그려 보세요.

Who am I?

1. I work at the hospital.

   I am a _____.

2. I work at school.

   I am a _____.

3. I work at the restaurant.

   I am a _____.

4. I work at the police station.

   I am a _____.

Where is my watch?

내 시계 어디 있지?

my watch

내 시계

my bag

내 가방

on the table

탁자 위에

under the desk

책상 아래에

Where is ~?

~는 어디 있지?

물건의 위치를 묻고 답할 수 있어요.

Where is my watch?

내 시계 어디 있지?

Where is my watch?

It's on the table.

탁자 위에 있어.

It's on the table.

Where is my bag?

내 가방 어디 있지?

Where is my bag?

It's under the desk.

책상 아래에 있어.

It's under the desk.

Where are you?

너 어디 있니?

a bathroom

화장실

a bedroom

침실

in

~ (안)에

in the bathroom

화장실에

in the bedroom

침실에

사람의 위치를 묻고 답할 수 있어요.

Where are you?

너 어디 있니?

Where are you?

I'm in the bathroom.

나 화장실에 있어.

I'm in the bathroom

Where's Mom?

Where's Mom?

엄마는 어디 계시니?

She's in the bedroom.

엄마는 침실에 계셔.

She's in the bedroom.

Tip. mom이 '우리 엄마'를 부르는 호칭일 때는 Mom으로 써요.

Rule 05. Preposition

A. 위치를 알려주는 말을 배워 보세요.

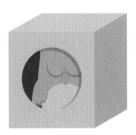

in the box
상자 안에

on the box
상자 위에

near the friend
친구 근처에

at the box
상자에

under the box
상자 아래에

over the box
상자를 넘어

B. 그림을 보고, 질문에 답하세요.

Where's the chicken?

It's _____ the roof.

Where's the goose?

It's _____ the yard.

Where's the horse?

It's _____ the tree.

Where's the pig?

It's _____ the mud.

 **Let's Have** *Fun!*

A. 잘 듣고, 빈칸에 알맞은 말을 쓰세요.

I'm late!
Dad, _____ is my bag?

It's _____ the sofa.

Oh, where's my jacket?

It's _____ your closet.

I got it.
_____ .

월   일

B. 주어진 문장에 알맞게 그림을 완성하세요.

1. The fish is in the fishbowl.   2. The dog is on the chair.

3. The cat is under the table.   4. The bird is at the window.

What are you doing?

너 뭐 하고 있니?

read

읽다

read a book

책을 읽다

make

만들다

make bubbles

비눗방울을 만들다

play mobile games

모바일 게임을 하다

지금 무엇을 하고 있는지 묻고 답할 수 있어요.

What are you doing?

너 뭐 하고 있니?

What are you doing?

I'm reading a book.

나 책 읽고 있어.

I'm reading a book

I'm making bubbles.

난 비눗방울을 만들고 있어.

I'm making bubbles

I'm playing mobile games.

난 모바일 게임을 하고 있어.

I'm playing mobile games.

What's he doing?

그는 뭐 하고 있니?

cook

요리하다

dinner

저녁(밥)

cook dinner

저녁밥을 요리하다

listen to

~을 (귀 기울여) 듣다, 귀 기울이다

music

음악

listen to music

음악을 듣다

다른 사람이 지금 하고 있는 일을 묻고 답할 수 있어요.

What's he doing?

그는 뭐 하고 있니?

What's he doing?

He's cooking dinner.

그는 저녁(밥)을 요리하고 있어.

He's cooking dinner

What's she doing?

그녀는 뭐 하고 있니?

What's she doing?

She's listening to music.

그녀는 음악을 듣고 있어.

She's listening to music.

I read.
나는 읽는다.

I am reading.
나는 읽고 있다.

She reads.
그녀는 읽는다.

She is reading.
그녀는 읽고 있다.

They read.
그들은 읽는다.

They are reading.
그들은 읽고 있다.

▶ 누가 지금 무엇을 하고 있는 중이라고 말할 때, 「am/is/are + 동사ing」를 써요.

A. 그림을 보고, 무엇을 하고 있는 중인지 쓰세요.

1.

read a book

She is reading a book

2.

play basketball

3.

watch TV

4.

talk

52

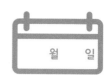

<동사에 ing를 붙이는 세 가지 방법>

방법 1. 대부분 동사는 그냥 끝에 ing를 붙여요.

read --> reading

방법 2. 동사가 e로 끝나면 e를 빼고 ing를 붙여요.

give --> giving

방법 3. 동사가 자음-모음-자음으로 끝나면 자음을 하나 더 쓰고 ing를 붙여요.

put --> putting

B. 주어진 동사에 알맞게 ing를 붙여 보세요.

take	cut	run	put	make
sit	swim	look	use	ride
catch	sleep	sing	play	write

동사 + ing	e를 빼고 + ing	마지막 자음 한 번 더 쓰고 + ing
looking	taking	cutting

Let's Have *Fun!*

A. 잘 듣고, 빈칸에 알맞은 말을 쓰세요.

Hi, Billy.
Where are you?

I'm [   ] my room.

Let's [   ] badminton.

Sorry, I can't. I'm busy.

What are you [   ]?

I'm [   ] a book.

B. 그림을 보고 질문에 답하세요.

smell the flowers

run

sit on the bench

play a ball

eat a sandwich

1. What is Jane doing?

➜ _____

2. What are Sue and Tim doing?

➜ _____

3. What is Mina doing?

➜ _____

4. What is Dad doing?

➜ _____

5. What is Paul doing?

➜ _____

What time is it?

몇 시니?

time

시간

o'clock

~시 (정확한 시간을 나타냄)

four

4, 넷

six

6, 여섯

nine

9, 아홉

ten

10, 열

twenty

20, 스물

시간을 묻고 답할 수 있어요.

What time is it?

몇 시니?

What time is it?

It's nine o'clock.

9시야.

It's nine o'clock.

It's four twenty.

4시 20분이야.

It's four twenty.

It's six ten.

It's six ten.

6시 10분이야.

Tip. 시간을 말할 때는 <It's+시+분>으로 표현해요. 때로는 It's 없이 <시+분>으로 말하기도 해요.

It's time for lunch.
점심 먹을 시간이야.

for

~을 위해, ~하러

time for

~을 할 시간

breakfast

아침(밥)

lunch

점심(밥)

dinner

저녁(밥)

무엇을 할 시간인지 말할 수 있어요.

It's eight o'clock.
8시야.

~~It's eight o'clock.~~

It's time for breakfast.
아침 먹을 시간이야.

~~It's time for breakfast.~~

It's twelve o'clock.
12시야.

~~It's twelve o'clock.~~

It's time for lunch.
점심 먹을 시간이야.

~~It's time for lunch.~~

Tip. 우리말은 아침밥도 '아침'이라고 말해요. 하지만 영어에서는 시간을 나타내는 '아침', '점심', '저녁'은 따로 있어요.
(morning 아침 - breakfast 아침(밥), noon 점심 - lunch 점심(밥), evening 저녁 - dinner 저녁(밥))

Rule 07. Telling Time

A. 시계를 보고, 시간을 말해 보세요.

01:21 It's one twenty-one.

02:05 It's two oh five.

03:10 It's three ten.

04:50 It's four fifty.

05:15 It's five fifteen.

06:30 It's six thirty.

07:00 It's seven o'clock.

08:35 It's eight thirty-five.

09:15 It's nine fifteen.

10:45 It's ten forty-five.

11:05 It's eleven oh five.

B. 시계를 보고, 영어로 답하세요.

What time is it?

1.

It's six twenty.

2.

_____

3.

_____

4.

_____

5.

_____

6.

_____

A. 잘 듣고, 빈칸에 알맞은 말을 쓰세요.

I'm hungry.
What [   ] is it?

It's only [   ] o'clock.

What's for [   ] today?

We're having curry and rice.

Oh, I love curry.
I can't wait.

Get your textbook.
[   ] time for class.

B. 나의 하루를 떠올리며, 시계와 문장을 완성하세요.

It's time for _____.

It's time for _____.

It's time for _____.

It's time for _____.

It's time for _____.

Do you want some pizza?

피자 좀 먹을래?

want

원하다, ~하고 싶어 하다

pizza

피자

cola

콜라

yes

응

no

아니

full

~이 가득한, 빈 공간이 없는

음식을 권하고 거기에 답할 수 있어요.

Do you want some pizza?

피자 좀 먹을래?

Do you want some pizza?

Yes, please.

Yes, please.

응, 줘.

No, thanks. I'm full.

아니, 괜찮아. 배불러.

No, thanks. I'm full.

Yes, I want pizza and cola.

응, 나는 피자와 콜라를 먹고 싶어.

Yes, I want pizza and cola.

Help yourself.

Help yourself.

마음껏 먹어.

65

What do you want?
무엇을 원하니?

ice cream

아이스크림

sure

확신하는

cold

추운

today

오늘

eat

~을 먹다

원하는 것을 묻고 답할 수 있어요.

What do you want?

무엇을 원하니?

What do you want?

I want some ice cream.

아이스크림 먹고 싶어.

I want some ice cream.

Are you sure? It's cold today.

정말이야? 오늘 추워.

Are you sure? It's cold today.

Yes, I am. I can eat it.

응. 먹을 수 있어.

Yes, I am. I can eat it.

Tip. can은 '~할 수 있다'의 뜻으로 뒤에 eat 같은 동사가 와요. 그래서 can eat은 '먹을 수 있다'입니다.

Rule 08. Conjunction

I want pizza and cola.

나는 피자와 콜라를 먹고 싶어.

I want pizza and she wants cola.

나는 피자를 먹고 싶어 하고 그녀는 콜라를 먹고 싶어 해.

▶ and는 '그리고'라는 뜻으로 두 문장을 연결하거나 문장 안의 두 부분을 연결해요.
두 부분 사이의 관계를 나타내어 문장을 더 잘 이해하도록 도와준답니다.

A. 다음 문장에서 두 부분을 연결하는 단어를 찾아 동그라미 하세요.

1. I have a book and a pencil.

2. Do you like a hamburger and a soda?

3. I like reading a book and singing a song.

4. You are very kind and help me a lot.

5. She wants to be a doctor and teacher.

I want pizza, but I don't want cola.

나는 피자는 먹고 싶지만 콜라는 먹고 싶지 않아.

▶ but는 '하지만'이라는 뜻으로 두 문장 또는 문장 안의 두 부분을 연결해요.
  앞의 것과 뒤의 것이 반대되는 말이거나 차이가 있음을 알려줘요.

B. 빈칸에 and 또는 but을 넣어 문장을 완성하세요.

1. I like cookies _____ I don't like bread.

2. Jane _____ I want chocolate ice cream.

3. I want to play outside, _____ it is raining.

4. Sam likes grapes _____ strawberries.

5. He eats a hamburger, _____ he doesn't drink a soda.

 **Let's Have *Fun!***

A. 잘 듣고, 빈칸에 알맞은 말을 쓰세요.

It smells good!
What are you cooking?

I'm making _____.
Do you _____ some pizza?

Yes, _____. I love pizza.
I'm thirsty.

I have cola, milk, _____
water.
What do you want?

I _____ cola. Thanks.

70

B. Free 칸에 자신이 원하는 것을 쓰고 짝과 함께 빙고 게임을 해요. (짝의 빙고는 131쪽에 있어요.)

a desk	a bag	a doll
a ship	Free	an airplane
apples	toys	loaves of bread

A: What do you want?

B: I want _____.

17 Is this your cup?

이거 네 컵이니?

월 일

a cup

컵

a ball

공

not

~ 아니다

your

너의

my

나의

mine

나의 것

물건의 소유를 묻고 답할 수 있어요.

Is this your cup?

이거 네 컵이니?

Is this your cup?

Yes, it's mine

Yes, it's mine.

응, 내 거야.

Is this your ball?

이거 네 거니?

Is this your ball?

No, it's not mine.
My ball is blue and white.

아니, 내 것이 아니야. 내 공은 파랑고 희어.

No, it's not mine.

My ball is blue and white

What's this?

이것은 무엇이니?

What's ~?

~는 무엇이니?

this is ~

이것은 ~이다

that is ~

저것은 ~이다

yours

너의 것

know

알다

a watch

(손목) 시계

궁금한 것을 묻고 답할 수 있어요.

What's this? Is this yours?

이것은 무엇이니? 이거 네 거니?

What's this? Is this yours?

No, I don't know.

아니, 나도 모르겠어.

No, I don't know.

What's that? Is that yours?

저것은 무엇이니? 저거 네 거니?

What's that? Is that yours?

Yes, it is. It's my watch.

응, 내 거야. 내 시계야.

Yes, it is. It's my watch.

Rule 09. Possessive

my 나의	**mine** 나의 것
your 너의	**yours** 너의 것
her 그녀의	**hers** 그녀의 것
his 그의	**his** 그의 것
our 우리의	**ours** 우리의 것
their 그들의	**theirs** 그들의 것

▶ 물건의 소유관계를 나타내는 단어를 **소유대명사**라고 해요.

A. 빈칸에 알맞은 말을 쓰세요.

1. I have the shoes.

➔ They are _____my_____ shoes.

➔ They are _____mine_____ .

2. You have the car.

➔ It is _____ car.

➔ It is _____ .

3. She has the books.

➜ They are _____ books.

➜ They are _____ .

4. He has the pencils.

➜ They are _____ pencils.

➜ They are _____ .

5. They have the house.

➜ It is _____ house.

➜ It is _____ .

6. We have the food.

➜ It is _____ food.

➜ It is _____ .

 **Let's Have Fun!**

A. 잘 듣고, 빈칸에 알맞은 말을 쓰세요.

Dad, did you see [____] gloves?

Well... I don't know.
Where are you [____]?

I'm going skating.

Are these [____] skates?

Oh, no. I borrow them from Jane.
They're [____].

Oh, I see.

월   일

B. 누구의 물건인지 분류해 보세요.

hers	his	theirs

What day is it today?

오늘은 무슨 요일이니?

day

날, 요일

today

오늘

Monday

월요일

Wednesday

수요일

Saturday

토요일

요일을 묻고 답할 수 있어요.

What day is it today?

오늘은 무슨 요일이니?

What day is it today?

It's Monday

It's Monday.

월요일이야.

It's Wednesday.

수요일이야.

It's Wednesday

It's Saturday

It's Saturday.

토요일이야.

Tip. 요일은 항상 대문자로 시작해요.

We have a math class today. 우리 오늘 수학 수업 있어.

Friday

금요일

have

(~을 가지고) 있다

like

~을 좋아하다

math

수학

a class

수업

과목을 말할 수 있어요.

What day is it today?

오늘 무슨 요일이야?

What day is it today?

It's Friday.

It's Friday.

금요일이야.

Good! We have a math class today.

좋아! 우리 오늘 수학 수업 있어.

Good! We have a math

class today.

Do you like math?

수학을 좋아하니?

Do you like math?

Yes, I do.

Yes, I do.

응, 좋아해.

 **Rule 10.** Months

A. 일 년 열두 달과 계절을 알아보세요.

SPRING 봄

March 3월

April 4월

May 5월

SUMMER 여름

June 6월

July 7월

August 8월

AUTUMN 가을

September 9월

October 10월

November 11월

WINTER 겨울

December 12월

January 1월

February 2월

B. 주어진 달의 지난달과 다음 달을 써 보세요.

LAST MONTH 지난달	THIS MONTH 이번 달	NEXT MONTH 다음 달
	October	
	November	
	December	
	August	
	February	
	June	
	April	

Tip. 요일처럼 달도 항상 대문자로 시작해요.

Let's Have *Fun!*

A. 잘 듣고, 빈칸에 알맞은 말을 쓰세요.

Dad! Are you done packing?

What are you talking about?

Today is _____!
It's a family trip _____.

No, it's not Saturday.

What? _____ day is it today?

It's _____.
Hurry up! You're late for school.

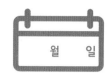

월 일

B. 자신만의 달력을 만들어 보세요.

How much is it?
이거 얼마예요?

How much ~?

얼마만큼, 어느 정도 ~니?

dollar

달러

I'll ~

나는 ~할 것이다 (I will의 줄임말)

take

가지고 가다

here

여기(남에게 무엇을 주거나 보여 줄 때)

가격을 묻고 답할 수 있어요.

How much is it?
이거 얼마예요?

How much is it?

It's twenty dollars.
20달러예요.

It's twenty dollars.

I'll take it.
이거 가져갈게요.

I'll take it.

Here you are.

Here you are.
여기요.

Tip. 2달러 (two dollars)부터는 dollars에 -s를 붙여요.

Can I help you?

도와줄까요?

Can I ~?

~해도 될까요?

help

~를 돕다

help you

너를 돕다

a sweater

스웨터

great

좋은, (크기 · 양이) 큰

도움을 제안하고 제안에 답할 수 있어요.

Can I help you?

도와줄까요?

Can I help you?

Yes, please. I want this sweater. How much is it?

네. 이 스웨터를 사고 싶어요. 이거 얼마예요?

Yes, please. I want this

sweater. How much is it?

It's nineteen dollars.

19달러예요.

It's nineteen dollars.

That's great! I'll take it.

좋네요! 그걸로 할게요.

That's great! I'll take it.

Rule 11. Money

one dollar

50 cents

25 cents
(quarter)

1 cent
(penny)

A. 동전을 세어 총 금액을 쓰세요.

1. ➜ total: $

2. ➜ total: $

3.  ➜ total: $

B. 질문에 답하세요.

$ 3.5

$ 1.75

$ 1.5

$ 5.25

Q: I want two notes and a ball.

How much is it?

A: _____.

 # Let's Have *Fun!*

A. 잘 듣고, 빈칸에 알맞은 말을 쓰세요.

Can I [   ] you?

Yes, please.
I'm looking for a pencil and a notebook.

How about this yellow pencil?

How [   ] is it?

It's fifty cents.

That's good. Do you have a notebook?

I recommend you this green one.
It's [   ] twenty-five.

Okay. I'll [   ] it.

B. 동전만으로 1달러가 되는 경우를 생각해 보세요.

1.

50 cents + 50 cents = 1 dollar

2.

3.

How's the weather today? 오늘 날씨는 어때?

weather

날씨

today

오늘

sunny

화창한

windy

바람이 부는

snowing

눈이 오는

날씨를 묻고 답할 수 있어요.

How's the weather today?

오늘 날씨는 어때?

How's the weather today?

It's sunny.

It's sunny.

화창해.

It's windy.

It's windy.

바람이 불어.

It's snowing.

It's snowing.

눈이 와.

Tip. 이때의 It's는 '그것은 ~이다'의 뜻이 아니에요. 날씨 문장을 말할 때 써 주는 말이랍니다.

What's the weather like in New York? 뉴욕 날씨는 어때?

like

~와 같은

in

(장소)에

raining

비가 오는

hot

더운

humid

습한, 눅눅한

cold

추운

장소에 따른 날씨를 묻고 말할 수 있어요.

What's the weather like in New York?

뉴욕 날씨는 어때?

What's the weather like

in New York?

It's raining.

It's raining.

비가 와.

It's hot and humid.

덥고 습해.

It's hot and humid

It's cold outside.

밖은 추워.

It's cold outside.

Tip. **What ~ like**는 **How**와 같은 뜻이에요.

Rule 12. Weather

sunny cloudy windy snowing

raining humid hot cold

A. 다음 단어의 알맞은 우리말 뜻을 아래에서 찾아 쓰세요.

1. sunny _____

2. cloudy _____

3. windy _____

4. snowing _____

5. raining _____

6. humid _____

7. hot _____

8. cold _____

| 구름이 많은 | 화창한 | 바람이 부는 | 비가 오는 |
| 눈이 내리는 | 더운 | 눅눅한 | 추운 |

B. 각 요일에 알맞은 날씨를 연결하세요.

Sunday

Monday

● It's raining

Tuesday

● It's cloudy.

Wednesday

● It's sunny.

Thursday

● It's windy.

Friday

● It's snowing.

Saturday

Let's Have *Fun!*

A. 잘 듣고, 빈칸에 알맞은 말을 쓰세요.

How's the [_____] today?

Look outside! It's [_____].

It's [_____] for building a snowman.

[_____] idea.
Go get your coat. Let's go outside.

Okay! It's exciting.
Did you see my gloves?

Don't be silly!
They're in your hand.

B. 지난 일주일 동안의 날씨를 완성하고, 오늘의 날씨에 대해 말해 보세요.

Day	Weather
Sunday	
Monday	
Tuesday	
Wednesday	
Thursday	
Friday	

A: How's the weather today?

B: It's _____ .

Did you have a good weekend?
지난 주말 잘 보냈니?

weekend

주말

Sunday

일요일

do

~하다

did

~했다

watch

보다

watched

보았다

good

좋은

지난 일에 대한 느낌을 말하고 답할 수 있어요.

Did you have a good weekend?

지난 주말 잘 보냈니?

Did you have a good

weekend?

Yes, I did.

Yes, I did.

응.

Did you have a good Sunday?

지난 일요일 잘 보냈니?

Did you have a good

Sunday?

Yes, I did. I watched TV.

응. 나는 TV 봤어.

Yes, I did. I watched TV.

What did you do yesterday? 너 어제 뭐 했니?

yesterday

어제

Saturday

토요일

play

(게임 · 놀이 등을) 하다

played

(게임 · 놀이 등을) 했다

go

가다

went

갔다

badminton

배드민턴

a park

공원

지난 일을 묻고 답할 수 있어요.

What did you do yesterday?

너 어제 뭐 했니?

What did you do yesterday?

I played badminton.

나는 배드민턴을 쳤어.

I played badminton.

What did you do on Saturday?

너 토요일에 뭐 했니?

What did you do on

Saturday?

I went to the park.

난 공원에 갔어.

I went to the park.

Rule 13. Past 1

I play badminton. 나는 배드민턴을 친다.

I played badminton. 나는 배드민턴을 쳤다.

▶ 지나간 일을 말할 때는 동사의 모양이 바뀌어요. 동사 뒤에 -d 또는 -ed를 붙이면 과거를 말하는 과거형 동사가 돼요.

A.다음 동사를 과거형으로 바꿔 보세요.

1. clean

2. help

3. dance

4. watch

5. stay

6. walk

7. learn

B. 다음 문장을 지나간 일을 말하는 과거형 문장으로 만드세요.

1. I play basketball.

➡ _____

2. We dance together.

➡ _____

3. They help the man.

➡ _____

4. I watch TV.

➡ _____

5. We clean our classroom.

➡ _____

109

Let's Have Fun!

A. 잘 듣고, 빈칸에 알맞은 말을 쓰세요.

Hi, Bori.
_____ you have a good weekend?

Yes, I did.

What did you _____ last weekend?

I _____ a soccer game at the stadium.

Was it exciting?

Yes, it was. Because my team won. How about you?

I _____ a movie.

월 일

B. 어제 내가 한 일을 그리고 질문에 답하세요.

A: What did you do yesterday?

B: _____.

vacation

방학

great

정말 좋은[기쁜]

fun

재미있는

is

~이다

was

~이었다

How was ~?

~은 어땠니?

과거의 경험에 대한 느낌을 묻고 답할 수 있어요.

How was your vacation?
방학 어땠어?

How was your vacation?

It was great

It was great.
매우 좋았어.

How about you, Andy?
앤디, 너는?

How about you, Andy?

It was fun.

It was fun.
재미있었어.

I had a great time.
좋은 시간을 보냈어.

have

~을 가지고 있다

had

~을 가졌다

meet

만나다

met

만났다

a trip

여행

many

많은

friend

친구

과거에 무엇을 했는지 말할 수 있어요.

How was your trip?
여행 어땠어?

How was your trip?

I had a great time.
좋은 시간을 보냈어.

I had a great time.

What did you do?
무엇을 했니?

What did you do?

I met many friends.
나는 많은 친구들을 만났어.

I met many friends.

Rule 14. Past 2

I go **to the concert.** 나는 콘서트에 간다.

I went **to the concert.** 나는 콘서트에 갔다.

▶ 지나간 일을 말할 때, 동사에 -d 또는 -ed를 붙여요. 하지만, 불규칙하게 변하는 동사들도 많아요.

A. 옆의 표를 보고, 질문에 알맞은 단어를 찾아보세요.

1. A와 B의 형태가 완전히 다른 단어는?

2. A와 B의 형태가 비슷한 단어는?

3. A와 B의 형태가 똑같은 단어는?

A(현재)	B(과거)	A(현재)	B(과거)
be	was / were	get	got
become	became	give	gave
begin	began	go	went
break	broke	grow	grew
bring	brought	have	had
buy	bought	hear	heard
catch	caught	hide	hid
choose	chose	hit	hit
come	came	hold	held
cut	cut	leave	left
do	did	make	made
draw	drew	meet	met
drink	drank	pay	paid
eat	ate	put	put
feel	felt	read [ri:d]	read [red]
find	found	run	ran
forget	forgot	say	said

Let's Have *Fun!*

A. 잘 듣고, 빈칸에 알맞은 말을 쓰세요.

Did you _____ a good vacation?

Yes, I did.
I _____ a great time.

What _____ you do?

I _____ my grandparents.

Where do they live?

They live in Busan.

It's far from Seoul.
How _____ Busan?

It's a nice city.

월 일

B. 각 동사를 과거형으로 말하며 목적지까지 가 보세요.

Start	become	break	bring	buy

catch | choose

come

give | get | draw | do | cut

have

hold

leave | make | meet | Finish

차 근 차 근

초등영어
교과서

정답 및 대본   미리쓰기

4학년

p.12

A. Make a sentence to ask about somebody's health.

1. How are you? 너 잘 지내니?

2. How is he? 그는 잘 지내니?

3. How are they? 그들은 잘 지내니?

4. How is she? 그녀는 잘 지내니?

p.13

B. Make a sentence to ask how to do something.

1. How do you sing? 너는 어떻게 노래하니?

2. How does he run? 그는 어떻게 달리니?

3. How does he study? 그는 어떻게 공부하니?

4. How do they walk? 그들은 어떻게 걷니?

p.14

A. Listen and fill in the blanks.

W: Hello. How are you? 안녕. 잘 지내니?

G: Great. Thanks. 좋아. 고마워.

W: I'd love you to meet my friend.
   내 친구를 소개할게.
   This is Tory. 이애는 토리야.

G: Hello. Nice to meet you. 안녕. 만나서 반가워.

B: Nice to meet you, too. 나도 만나서 반가워.

p.20

A. Find a verb in the sentence.

1. James eats a pizza. ➜ eats
   제임스는 피자를 먹는다.

2. Hans laughs loudly. ➜ laughs
   한스는 크게 웃는다.

3. My family goes to church. ➜ goes
   우리 가족은 교회에 간다.

4. Suho plays the violin. ➜ plays
   수호는 바이올린을 연주한다.

5. Jina sings a song every day. ➜ sings
   지나는 매일 노래를 부른다.

B. (예시)

study   sit   stand   eat   sleep wash
talk   listen   eat   watch   cook
read   play   meet   dance   sing

at school

at home

run   play   ride   order   eat   wait
           meet   talk   pay

at a park

at a restaurant

p.22

A. Listen and fill in the blanks.

G: Let's play soccer. 축구하자.

B: Sounds good. 좋아.

W: Sorry, I can't. 미안하지만 난 못해.
   I have a cold. 감기에 걸렸어.

B: That's too bad. 안됐구나.

G: I hope you get well soon. 금방 낫길 바라.

p.23

		¹b					
²b	a	d	m	i	n	t	o	n
		s					
		k					
		e					
		t					
		b					
		a					
³b	a	⁴s	e	b	a	l	l
		o				l	
		c					
		c					
		e					
		r					

p.28

1. Wash — the book.

2. Study — your face.

3. Read — English every day.

4. Clean up — to school.

5. Go — the table.

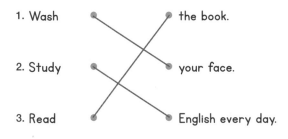

p.29

B. Change the sentence to a prohibition.

1. Don't wash your face. 얼굴을 닦지 마.

2. Don't study English every day.
   매일 영어 공부를 하지 마.

3. Don't read the book. 그 책을 읽지 마.

4 Don't clean up the table. 그 탁자를 치우지 마.

5. Don't go to school. 학교에 가지 마.

p.30

A. Listen and fill in the blanks.

W: People make this park dirty.
   사람들이 공원을 더럽히네.

M: Let's <u>clean</u> up. 치우자.

   Help me, please. 나 좀 도와줘.

W: Okay. I'll <u>help</u>. 응. 도울게.

M: Thanks. <u>Put</u> the paper cups here.
   고마워. 종이컵은 여기에 둬.

W: Don't touch these bottles. They're broken.
   이 병들은 만지지 마. 깨졌어.

M: I can handle it. 내가 처리할 수 있어.

W: <u>Don't</u> do that. We need gloves.
   하지 마. 우리는 장갑이 필요해.

p.31

B. Look and match.

1. ⓔ 공책을 펴라!
2. ⓒ 칠판으로 가라!
3. ⓕ 손을 들어라!
4. ⓓ 앉아라!
5. ⓐ 조용히 해라!
6. ⓑ 휴대전화기는 가방에 둬라!

p.37

1. an airport
   공항

2. a school
   학교

3. a police station
   경찰서

4. a fire station
   소방서

5. an animal hospital
   동물병원

p.38

A. Listen and fill in the blanks.

W: <u>Look</u>! I can't believe he is here.
   봐! 그가 여기 있다니 믿을 수 없어.

M: Who? Do you mean the guy surrounded
   by the girls? 누구? 여자애들에 둘러싸인 남자 말이니?

W: <u>Yes</u>. He's looking at me. 응. 그가 날 보고 있어.

M: Well, I don't thinks so. 글쎄. 그건 아닌 것 같아.

   <u>Who</u> is he? 그는 누구니?

W: Don't you know Tom? 너 톰을 몰라?

   He's a famous <u>musician</u>. 그는 유명한 음악가야.

p.39

B. Guess and draw.

1. I work at the hospital. 나는 병원에서 일해.

   I am a <u>nurse/doctor</u>. 나는 간호사/의사야.

2. I work at school. 나는 학교에서 일해.

   I am a <u>teacher</u>. 나는 선생님이야.

3. I work at the restaurant. 나는 레스토랑에서 일해.

   I am a <u>cook/waiter</u>. 나는 요리사/웨이터야.

4. I work at the police station. 나는 경찰서에서 일해.

   I am a <u>police officer</u>. 나는 경찰관이야.

p.45

B. Look and answer the question.

Where's the chicken? 닭은 어디 있니?
It's <u>on</u> the roof. 지붕 위에 있어.

Where's the goose? 거위는 어디 있니?
It's <u>in</u> the yard. 마당에 있어.

Where's the horse? 말은 어디 있니?
It's <u>under</u> the tree. 나무 아래에 있어.

Where's the pig? 돼지는 어디 있니?
It's <u>in</u> the mud. 진흙 속에 있어.

p.46

A. Listen and fill in the blanks.

G: I'm late! 늦었어요.

   Dad, <u>where</u> is my bag? 아빠, 내 가방 어딨어요?

M: It's <u>on</u> the sofa. 소파 위에 있어.

G: Oh, where is my jacket? 아, 내 재킷은 어딨어요?

M: It's <u>in</u> your closet. 네 옷장에 있어.

G: I got it! <u>Thanks</u>. 알았어요! 고마워요.

p.47

B. Draw a picture to match.

1. The fish is in the fishbowl. 물고기가 어항에 있다.

2. The dog is on the chair. 개가 의자 위에 있다.

3. The cat is under the table. 고양이가 탁자 아래에 있다.

4. The bird is at the window. 새가 창가에 있다.

p.52

A. Look at the picture and make a present continuous sentence.

1. She is reading a book. 그녀는 책을 읽고 있다.

2. He is playing basketball. 그는 농구를 하고 있다.

3. They are watching TV. 그들은 텔레비전을 보고 있다.

4. They are talking. 그들은 이야기하고 있다.

p.53

동사 + ing	e를 빼고 + ing	마지막 자음 한번 더 쓰고 + ing
looking	taking	cutting
catching	using	sitting
sleeping	making	swimming
singing	riding	running
playing	writing	putting

p.54

A. Listen and fill in the blanks.

W: Hi, Billy. Where are you? 안녕, 빌리. 너 어디 있니?

M: I'm <u>in</u> my room. 내 방에 있어.

W: Let's <u>play</u> badminton. 배드민턴 치자.

M: Sorry, I can't. I'm busy. 미안하지만 안 돼. 나 바빠.

W: What are you <u>doing</u>? 뭐 하고 있니?

M: I'm <u>reading</u> a book. 책을 읽고 있어.

p.55

B. Look and answer the questions.

1. What is Jane doing? 제인은 무엇을 하고 있니?

➔ She is sitting on the bench. 그녀는 벤치에 앉아 있어.

2. What are Sue and Tim doing?
   수와 팀은 무엇을 하고 있니?

➔ They are playing a ball. 그들은 공놀이를 하고 있어.

3. What is Mina doing? 미나는 무엇을 하고 있니?

➔ She is smelling the flowers.
   그녀는 꽃향기를 맡고 있어.

4. What is Dad doing? 아빠는 무엇을 하고 있니?

➔ He is running. 그는 달리고 있어.

5. What is Paul doing? 폴은 무엇을 하고 있니?

➔ He is eating a sandwich. 그는 샌드위치를 먹고 있어.

p.60

A. Look and tell time.

It's one twenty-one. 1시 21분이야.

It's two oh five. 2시 5분이야.

It's three ten. 3시 10분이야.

It's four fifty. 4시 50분이야.

It's five fifteen. 5시 15분이야.

It's six thirty. 6시 30분이야.

It's seven o'clock. 7시야.

It's eight thirty-five. 8시 35분이야.

It's nine fifteen. 9시 15분이야.

It's ten forty-five. 10시 45분이야.

It's eleven oh five. 11시 5분이야.

p.61

B. Look and answer in English.

1. It's six twenty. 6시 20분이야.

2. It's ten thirty-five. 10시 35분이야.

3. It's seven o'clock. 7시야.

4. It's twelve forty. 12시 40분이야.

5. It's two fifteen. 2시 15분이야.

6. It's one thirty. / It's half past one.
   1시 30분이야. / 1시 반이야.

p.62

A. Listen and fill in the blanks.

M: I'm hungry. 배고프다.

   What <u>time</u> is it? 몇 시야?

W: It's only <u>eleven</u> o'clock. 아직 11시야.

M: What's for <u>lunch</u> today? 오늘 점심은 뭐야?

W: We're having curry and rice.
   우리는 카레라이스를 먹을 거야.

M: Oh, I love curry. 아, 나 카레 진짜 좋아해.

   I can't wait. 참을 수가 없네.

W: Get your textbook. 교과서 꺼내.

   <u>It's</u> time for class. 수업 시간이야.

p.63

B. Complete the sentence.

It's time for <u>breakfast</u>. 아침 먹을 시간이야.

It's time for <u>school</u>. 학교 갈 시간이야.

It's time for <u>studying</u>. 공부할 시간이야.

It's time for <u>lunch</u>. 점심 먹을 시간이야.

It's time for <u>bed</u>. 잘 시간이야.

p.68

A. Circle the conjunction in the sentence.

1. I have a book (and) a pencil.
   나는 책과 연필이 있어.

2. Do you like a hamburger (and) a soda?
   너는 햄버거와 탄산음료 좋아하니?

125

3. I like reading a book (and) singing a song.
나는 책 읽기와 노래 부르기를 좋아해.

4. You are very kind (and) help me a lot.
너는 정말 친절하고 나를 많이 도와줘.

5. She wants to be a doctor (and) teacher.
그녀는 의사와 선생님이 되고 싶어 해.

p.69

B. Fill in the blank with "and" or "but".

1. I like cookies, but I don't like bread.
나는 쿠키는 좋아하지만, 빵은 안 좋아해.

2. Jane and I want chocolate ice cream.
제인과 나는 초콜릿 아이스크림을 원해.

3. I want to play outside, but it is raining.
나는 밖에서 놀고 싶지만, 비가 와.

4. Sam likes grapes and strawberries.
샘은 포도와 딸기를 좋아해.

5. He eats a hamburger, but he doesn't drink a
soda. 그는 햄버거를 먹지만, 탄산음료는 안 먹어.

p.70

A. Listen and fill in the blanks.

W: It smells good! 냄새 좋다!
What are you cooking? 뭐 요리하고 있니?

M: I'm making pizza. 피자를 만들고 있어.
Do you want some pizza? 피자 좀 먹을래?

W: Yes, please. I love pizza. 응, 줘. 나 피자 정말 좋아해.
I'm thirsty. 목마르다.

M: I have cola, milk, and water. 콜라, 우유, 물이 있어.
What do you want? 무엇을 원하니?

W: I want cola. Thanks. 콜라 줘. 고마워.

p.76

A. Complete the sentence.

1. I have the shoes. 나는 신발이 있어.
They are my shoes. 그것들은 내 신발이야.
They are mine. 그것들은 내 거야.

2. You have the car. 너는 차가 있어.
It is your car. 그것은 네 차야.

It is yours. 그것은 네 거야.

3. She has the books. 그녀는 책이 있어.
They are her books. 그것들은 그녀의 책이야.
They are hers. 그것들은 그녀의 것이야.

4. He has the pencils. 그는 연필이 있어.
They are his pencils. 그것들은 그의 연필이야.
They are his. 그것들은 그의 것이야.

5. They have the house. 그들은 집이 있어.
It is their house. 그것은 그들의 집이야.
It is theirs. 그것은 그들의 것이야.

6. We have the food. 우리는 음식이 있어.
It is our food. 그것은 우리의 음식이야.
It is ours. 그것은 우리 것이야.

p.78

A. Listen and fill in the blanks.

W: Dad, did you see my gloves?
아빠, 내 장갑 보셨어요?

M: Well... I don't know. 글쎄, 모르겠다.
Where are you going? 너 어디 가니?

W: I'm going skating. 스케이트 타러 가요.

M: Are these your skates? 이것들이 네 스케이트니?

W: Oh, no. I borrow them from Jane.
아, 아니요. 저는 제인한테 그것들은 빌려요.
They're hers. 그것들은 그녀의 것이에요.

M: Oh, I see. 아, 알겠다.

p.79

B. Sort the things.

hers	his	theirs
toys	a pencil	
a cat	a notebook	
a bike	a bag	apples
cookies	candies	
apples	apples	

126

p.85

B. Fill in the table.

LAST MONTH 지난달	THIS MONTH 이번 달	NEXT MONTH 다음 달
September	October	November
October	November	December
November	December	January
July	August	September
January	February	March
May	June	July
March	April	May

p.86

A. Listen and fill in the blanks.

W: Dad! Are you done packing? 아빠, 짐 다 싸셨어요?

M: What are you talking about? 무슨 말이니?

W: Today is <u>Saturday</u>! 오늘 토요일이에요!

　It's a family trip <u>day</u>. 가족 여행 가는 날이요.

M: No, it's not Saturday. 아냐, 오늘은 토요일이 아니야.

W: What? <u>What</u> day is it today?

　뭐라고요? 오늘 무슨 요일인데요?

M: It's <u>Friday</u>. 금요일이야.

　Hurry up! You're late for school.

　서둘러! 너 학교 늦었어.

p.92

A. Count money.

1. **1.25**

2. **0.76**

3. **1.01**

p.93

B. Answer the question.

A: I want two notebooks and a ball.

　나는 공책 두 권과 공 하나를 원해요.

　How much is it? 얼마예요?

B: <u>It's eight seventy-five(8.75) dollars.</u>

　8.75 달러예요.

p.94

A. Listen and fill in the blanks.

M: Can I <u>help</u> you? 도와줄까요?

W: Yes, please. 네.

　I'm looking for a pencil and a notebook.

　연필과 공책을 찾고 있어요.

M: How about this yellow pencil?

　이 노란색 연필 어때요?

W: How <u>much</u> is it? 얼마예요?

M: It's fifty cents. 50센트예요.

W: That's good. Do you have a notebook?

　좋네요. 공책 있어요?

M: I recommend you this green one.

　이 초록색 공책을 추천해요.

　It's <u>one</u> twenty-five. 1.25달러예요.

W: Okay. I'll <u>take</u> it. 네. 그걸로 할게요.

p.95

B. (예시)

1. 50 cents + 50 cents

2.   25 cents + 25 cents + 50 cents

3.

25 cents + 25 cents + 25 cents + 25 cents

p.100

A. Match a word and its meaning.

1. sunny – 화창한

2. cloudy – 구름이 많은

3. windy – 바람이 부는

4. snowing – 눈이 내리는

5. raining – 비가 오는

6. humid – 눅눅한

7. hot – 더운

8. cold – 추운

p.101

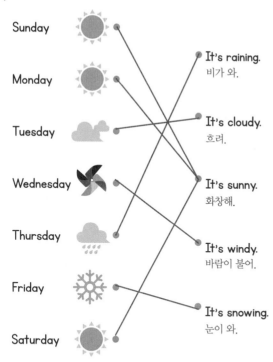

Sunday

Monday

Tuesday

Wednesday

Thursday

Friday

Saturday

It's raining.
비가 와.

It's cloudy.
흐려.

It's sunny.
화창해.

It's windy.
바람이 불어.

It's snowing.
눈이 와.

p.102

A. Listen and fill in the blanks.

M: How's the <u>weather</u> today? 오늘 날씨 어때?

W: Look outside! It's <u>snowing</u>. 밖을 봐! 눈 와.

M: It's <u>time</u> for building a snowman.
눈사람 만들 시간이야.

W: <u>Good</u> idea. Go get your coat. Let's go

outside. 좋은 생각이야. 코트 입어. 밖에 나가자.

M: Okay! It's exciting. Did you see my gloves?
좋아! 신난다. 내 장갑 봤니?

W: Don't be silly! They're in your hand.
바보같이 굴지 마! 네 손에 있잖아.

p.108

A. Change the verb from present to past.

1. clean - cleaned 청소하다 - 청소했다

2. help - helped 돕다 - 도왔다

3. dance - danced 춤추다 - 춤췄다

4. watch - watched 보다 - 봤다

5. stay - stayed 머무르다 - 머물렀다

6. walk - walked 걷다 - 걸었다

7. learn - learned 배우다 - 배웠다

p.109

B. Change a sentence to past tense.

1. I play basketball. 나는 농구를 한다.

➜ I played basketball. 나는 농구를 했다.

2. We dance together. 우리는 함께 춤을 춘다.

➜ We danced together. 우리는 함께 춤을 췄다.

3. They help the man. 그들은 그 남자를 돕는다.

➜ They helped the man. 그들은 그 남자를 도왔다.

4. I watch TV. 나는 텔레비전을 본다.

➜ I watched TV. 나는 텔레비전을 봤다.

5. We clean our classroom. 우리는 교실을 청소한다.

➜ We cleaned our classroom. 우리는 교실을 청소했다.

p.110

A. Listen and fill in the blanks.

W: Hi, Bori. 안녕, 보리야.

<u>Did</u> you have a good weekend? 주말 잘 보냈니?

M: Yes, I did. 응, 잘 보냈어.

W: What did you <u>do</u> last weekend?
지난 주말에 뭐했어?

M: I <u>watched</u> a soccer game at the stadium.
경기장에서 축구 경기 봤어.

W: Was it exciting? 재미있었어?

M: Yes, it was. Because my team won.
응, 재미있었어. 왜냐하면 우리 팀이 이겼거든.

How about you? 너는 어땠니?

W: I <u>saw</u> a movie. 난 영화를 봤어.

p.116

A. Look at the table, and then answer the
question.

1. be-was/were, bring-brought, buy-bought,
catch-caught, go-went, leave-left, do-did,
eat-ate, pay-paid, say-said

2. become-became, begin-began, break-broke, choose-chose, come-came, draw-drew, drink-drank, feel-felt, find-found, forget-forgot, get-got, give-gave, grow-grew, have-had, hear-heard, hide-hid, hold-held, make-made, meet-met, run-ran

3. cut-cut, hit-hit, put-put, read-read(read는 현재와 과거가 발음이 달라요.)

p.118

A. Listen and fill in the blanks.

W: Did you <u>have</u> a good vacation? 방학 잘 보냈니?

M: Yes, I did. 응, 잘 보냈어.

   I <u>had</u> a great time. 나는 좋은 시간을 보냈어.

W: What <u>did</u> you do? 뭐 했어?

M: I <u>met</u> my grandparents.
   나는 우리 할아버지 할머니를 만났어.

W: Where do they live? 그분들은 어디 사셔?

M: They live in Busan. 그분들은 부산에 사셔.

W: It's far from Seoul. 서울에서 멀구나.

   How <u>was</u> Busan? 부산은 어땠어?

M: It's a nice city. 멋진 도시야.

빙고 게임 방법

1. Free 칸을 채워 각자의 빙고 판을 완성해요.
2. 가위바위보로 순서를 정해요.
3. 진 사람이 What do you want? 라고 묻고 이긴 사람은 I want ~.라고 답하며 자신의 빙고 칸을 지워요.
4. 차례 대로 역할을 바꿔가며 진행해요.
5. 빙고 판에 온전한 한 줄을 먼저 지우는 사람이 이겨요.

BINGO

an airplane	a ship	a doll
toys	Free	a desk
apples	a bag	loaves of bread

A: What do you want?

B: I want _____.

주니어 영어 낭독 훈련 시리즈

박광희 • 캐나다 교사 영낭훈 연구팀 지음 | 대국판 | 12,000원 | MP3 CD 1

주니어 영어 낭독 훈련 Picture Talk ❶ | 주니어 영어 낭독 훈련 Picture Talk ❷

주니어 영어 낭독 훈련 Topic Talk ❶ | 주니어 영어 낭독 훈련 Topic Talk ❷

낭독과 회화 훈련을 동시에!
스피킹 기본기를 체득하고 싶은 주니어를 위한 영어 낭독 훈련 교재

주니어 영어 낭독 훈련 『I Can Talk』 시리즈는 집과 학교에서 접할 수 있는 생활 모습들과 취미, 여가생활에 관한 내용들을 영어로 설명하고 대화하는 훈련을 단계별로 실천함으로써 영어 회화의 첫 걸음을 뗄 수 있습니다.

『I Can Talk』 시리즈로 영어 낭독을 하면서 입을 열어 보세요.

Level	Picture Talk 사진 보며 말하기	Topic Talk 주제에 대해 말하기
입문 Beginner	**Picture Talk 1** 집과 학교에서 접할 수 있는 생활 모습을 생생하게 포착한 20장의 사진들을 영어로 설명하고, 대화하는 훈련을 합니다.	**Topic Talk 1** Picture Talk 1과 관련된 주제에 대해 일관성과 연계성을 가진 텍스트를 가지고 스피킹을 효과적으로 학습합니다.
기초 Basic	**Picture Talk 2** 취미 또는 여가생활에 관한 모습을 생생하게 포착한 20장의 사진들을 영어로 설명하고, 대화하는 훈련을 합니다.	**Topic Talk 2** Picture Talk 2와 관련된 주제에 대해 일관성과 연계성을 가진 텍스트를 가지고 스피킹을 효과적으로 학습합니다.